HOW TO MAKE

A BUDGET

AGNES MCCOY

TABLE OF CONTENTS

INTRODUCTION

How do you feel when you read one of the many articles outlining how much you need in your pension pot in order to have a comfortable retirement? Or how about the articles informing us that we will need to work till we drop down dead? I know – utterly depressed!

This little book is written primarily for those of us who either have small private or workplace pensions, or will be reliant on their state pension only. That being said I am hoping that it will have a wider appeal to anyone approaching retirement regardless of their financial situation because my aim is to point you in the direction of widening your horizons, finding a new purpose in life and ensuring you have the most fun possible in the coming years no matter what your budget is.

When the vast majority of us are slaving away at the coalface in order to keep body and soul together we often do not have much time to focus on ourselves, what we really enjoy doing or what it is that gives us a sense of purpose and fulfillment. For those of us who loved our jobs and found our fulfillment and purpose there then retirement can leave us feeling lost because our work defined who we are.

Regardless of which camp you fall into, now is the time to become proactive and get excited about the next phase of your life.

I have to tell you upfront that I do not intend to go into huge detail with all that we discuss in this book. I am going to put the ideas out there and allow you to do all the research needed for your circumstances. Developing your curiosity and your creativity will pay huge dividends in making the best use of your time. We will look at money – how to best manage it, cut your costs, make more of it and ensure that you are receiving all that you are entitled to. I hope to show you that you do not need very deep pockets in order to have an interesting and fulfilling life.

We will spend time on how you can discover the things that you truly value as well as the things you enjoy doing most and how giving your time to help other people or causes will provide you with a much deeper form of happiness than accumulating endless materialistic stuff.

Lastly, we will look at ways to improve your health and wellbeing in a fairly relaxed manner so that you are fit to enjoy all the good times to come.

It is time to jump out of your rut – be curious, suss out all the information you need and find out what it is that really lights you up. That is what this book is all about so let's get started.

CHAPTER 1
MONEY MONEY MONEY
(PART ONE)

For most of us money plays a central role in our lives. It dictates how hard we have to work, the type of area and house that we live in, where we holiday, what type of car we drive and so on. Money is essential for survival but does the meaning we attach to money give it too much power where enjoyment of life is concerned?

If our basic needs are met – food, shelter, clothing, the ability to pay our bills and afford some luxuries you would think we could be quite content with that. For many of us that is just not so. Our whole economy is built on us acquiring more and more. Some people own so much stuff they need to rent storage units to hold it. Not only do we want to keep up with the Jones – we want to outdo them in every way! If we get a pay rise or bonus, we do not save it for a rainy day – instead we upgrade our car or plan a home extension. In this way we live up to every penny we earn and studies show that no matter what level of income we have we think that we would feel prosperous and happy if we could just acquire double that amount. This mindset leads us to feel that we never have enough and, if we are intent on bigger houses, better cars, more exotic holidays, designer label clothes, shoes and bags etc. etc. then not only can It lead us into a downward spiral of debt and worry but we will also fail to tune into our true values and will be unable to live a more spiritual purpose filled life. We will certainly be the person who knows the price of everything and the value of nothing.

For others money represents not so much the constant procurement of material goods but rather security. They feel the need to have X number of pounds in the bank – just in case! However, we must realize that having security in this life is almost unobtainable. A financial crash could render most of our assets worthless. Ill health, accidents, the breakdown of relationships – all sorts of misfortune can befall any one of us at any time so, is there any point in us placing our trust in money as iron-clad security? We have all probably heard of some unfortunate individual who slaved away all their working life in a hated job only to fall into ill-health and die shortly after they retired.

Another mindset that some people have where money is concerned is that of the miser. These people cannot enjoy their money at all because, no matter how much they own, they are terrified of losing it all and being left destitute. They cannot be generous to either themselves or anyone else but, unfortunately, they can be sure that after they have shuffled off this mortal coil, there will be a queue of others only too willing to spend it for them! As the saying goes, where there's a will there's a relative.

Therefore, it is very important to work out what our true values in life are and figure out how our attitude to money relates to these values. One of the rules of a peaceful life is to spend less money than we take in. If we live our life by this rule, we can banish worry and stress as far as our finances are concerned. As I have said earlier, capitalism is built on the premise of acquiring more and more stuff. We need to keep buying and spending in order to keep the wheels of the economy moving. This has led, not only to difficulties for us as individuals, but the planet we live on is now in serious trouble. We are stripping the Earth of natural resources and we are polluting the environment irrevocably with our behavior. We need to ask ourselves whether we really need all the stuff and expensive experiences, and also ask do they make us truly happy?

Pick a time when you can concentrate without distractions and sit down with a pen and paper. Take your time to really think about the following questions and answer them as honestly as possible.

1. Who and what are the most important things in my life?

2. Who do I most like to spend my time with and what are the enjoyable things we do together?

3. When all work and chores are done what is my favourite way to spend my leisure time?

4. What is it that really interests and fascinates me?

5. In what area would I like to make a difference in the world?

6. What have I given up that I used to love doing or what is it that I've never done but would really like to try?

7. If money was absolutely no object what would I be doing?

If you take time to think about the answers to these questions, I am sure you will be able to see that the most valuable things in your life cannot be bought with money and you should also realize that you can absolutely have a very interesting, purposeful and happy life without the need for millions in the bank. That last question often stumps people. If you ask someone what they would do if they won the lottery, they will tell you of their plans for a new house, luxurious holiday, top of the range car and making their families financially secure. After that they have no idea how they are going to spend their time – and we all know that sitting on a beautiful beach for six months would become excruciatingly boring for most people.

Maybe you have dreamed of going on a luxurious cruise and have managed to make it happen. Did it honestly live up to your expectations? Often the idea of the holiday is much better than the actual holiday. Or perhaps you hankered after a two-carat diamond ring and you received it for a special birthday but after a while the novelty wears off and your enjoyment diminishes.

This tells us that being overly materialistic can never bring us true fulfillment and we must therefore become pro-active in building the interesting and enjoyable life that we perhaps did not have time for when we were working hard at the coalface and providing for our families.

CHAPTER 2
MONEY MONEY MONEY
(PART TWO)

In this chapter we will explore the practicalities of our finances. First, let me say that if you have not already made friends with the internet then now would be a good time to do so. The internet can provide you with so much useful information – such as the lowdown on all the benefits and discounts you ae entitled to, free courses, price comparison sites, voucher codes, how to invest your money, ways to make extra cash, free exercise tutorials – the list is almost endless. If you do not have internet access at home, and not everyone does, check out your local library. They frequently run free courses on how to use the internet too which is a win- win scenario!

You now need to work out all your income and outgoings, any savings or pension pots you may have and you also need to find out whether you are entitled to any benefits such as pension credits. If you have a financial adviser you can work with them to make the most of all your assets. If you have to access this information yourself, check out government websites or contact Citizens Advice – they can help you with all this and more.

Do you still have a mortgage or other debts? If so, you will have to come up with plan to pay them down. You could consider continuing to work on a part-time basis. If you feel that it would be unbearable to continue any longer in your present job then think of some type of work which is more in line with your interests. For example, if you love fashion look for a job in a boutique or if you are really into DIY then consider some of the large hardware stores who actively seek out more senior members of society as employees.

Another option might be to downsize to a smaller property. This would have the added advantage of a reduction in costs for property taxes, insurance and maintenance etc.

If you really want to stay in your current home and you have a workplace or private pension, you might be able to put your tax-free lump sum towards paying down your debt.

If this is not an option think of ways you could generate income from your home by, for example, taking a lodger or renting rooms on a B&B basis. Do make sure you check out the tax implications of any of these ideas and also check that any extra income you earn will not affect any benefits you receive.

Go through your bank statements every month. Are you paying any direct debits for something you no longer use but have forgotten to cancel? Are you paying for TV packages that you either do not watch very often or do not enjoy very much? Perhaps you could find enough entertaining programs on free-to-view platforms such as BBCiplayer or More4. You need to ensure that every penny you spend is worthwhile.

Keep a note of the dates any utility or insurance contracts are due for renewal. Never renew these automatically – always shop around for lower prices. This is where internet comparison sites can be so helpful in getting the best value for money. Again, if you are not confident with using technology then rope in someone who is – it will be well worth your while.

Keep a spending diary for a month and record absolutely everything you spend money on. Go through this with a fine-tooth comb and identify where you are spending needlessly. This is not about giving up everything you love but rather working out what your non-negotiables are. One example might illustrate this. I have seen a well-known chain of restaurants offering a cup of tea and a cookie for £1.85 and, maybe if you are in town, you would consider taking advantage of this offer. If, instead you wait for half an hour until you get home, think about how many cups of tea and cookies you could make for £1.85. This might seem an insignificant sum but it all adds up and you want to make sure you get full enjoyment for all your spending.

Work out a budget for yourself. Make a list of all your essential outgoings – utilities, mortgage or rent, insurances, food, car or travel expenses etc. Add these together and divide by 12 or 52 depending on whether you work on a monthly or weekly basis. This gives you the amount that you need to put aside each month or week for expenses. After that, aim to put an amount aside as savings. You could divide this into smaller amounts that you put aside for different categories such as Christmas, holidays, weddings etc. It would be an excellent idea to put aside a sum, no matter how small, that you do not touch. This can build up as a cushion for a rainy day.

Look at the things you spend money on. For example, do you like to eat out quite often? Which element of eating out is it that you enjoy most? Is it the fine foods and wine, or is it the convivial company of family or friends that brings you most pleasure? If it is the latter then consider more economical ways of meeting up. You could meet up for lunch instead of dinner in the evening or you could arrange a picnic somewhere scenic if the weather is nice. If it really is the food and wine that you enjoy most then cut back on the number of times you go – you will appreciate the experience much more if it is a real treat. Learn to cook well now that you have more free time on your hands and invite your friends round to enjoy your culinary delights which will cost a lot less than eating out. Perhaps a group of you could take it in turns to host dinner – this would be both more economical and very sociable

Many people spend a sizeable chunk of their money on holidays and travel. Again, examine what it is about your vacations that you really love. Is it the change of routine, is it discovering new cultural experiences in your chosen destination or do you just love relaxing in the sun? Get creative and work out ways that you can holiday for less. As a senior citizen there will be lots of discounts available to you and, most likely, you can travel in the low season when prices can be considerably lower. Instead of going abroad two or three times each year consider going once for a longer period and explore staycations the rest of the year. This also helps to cut down your carbon footprint and also gives a boost to the tourist industry closer to home. Another advantage of a staycation is that it cuts down on the hassle involved in travelling these days which helps to make your break much more relaxing.

You could think of house-swapping or you could register with a housesitting company and stay in lovely places in exchange for looking after a pet or doing some light housework.

Adopt this mindset with all aspects of your day to day living costs. Turn frugality into a hobby and figure out how you can have the essence of all the things you enjoy without paying over the odds. Invite friends round for games nights instead of meeting up at the pub – another example of how you can cut down on your expenditure whilst still having lots of fun.

Maybe you need to get your hands on extra cash to save for something special. You could take on a part-time job for the duration or you could look online for some side hustle ideas. Do you have some skills that you could teach others? This could be done as an online tutorial or in a normal classroom type of setting. Check with your local University of the Third Age – they may well want to run a class using your expertise. You could set up a dog-walking service or use your calligraphy skills to write wedding invitations. Put your thinking cap on and you will be surprised with the ideas you can come up with.

I hope this chapter has been beneficial in not only helping you to take control of your finances, but in also opening your mind to examples of the many different ways you can cut down on spending while still having a very full and enjoyable life

Chapter 3
What To Do With Myself

You can retire from a job but don't ever retire from making extremely meaningful contributions in life – a quote from Stephen Covey.

We may or may not have enjoyed our working lives but at least work did fill up our time and gave us a reason to get out of bed in the morning – even if this was just to earn the money necessary for keeping body and soul together. But, either way, if we have not developed interests and activities in our leisure time then retirement can be a shock to the system. What do we do now? And this can be furthered complicated if we have a modest budget to work with. However, having an enjoyable, interesting and fulfilling retirement does not require a huge income.

In an earlier chapter you answered questions which tried to uncover your true values and interests. Have a look over your answers again and make two lists. On the first list write down all the activities you enjoy now, have enjoyed in the past or have always felt drawn to but have never tried. Try to get a good mix here. Include some that stretch you physically – e.g., walking, cycling, swimming, dancing, some that stretch you mentally – e.g., reading, learning a new language, writing a book, doing crosswords, and some which are sociable – e.g., bridge clubs, knitting circles, choirs, men's shed. Also, include some things that you do purely for relaxation – e.g., watching T.V., meditating or enjoying a cup of coffee while you read the papers.

You may feel drawn to certain pursuits but feel intimidated by the thought of giving them a try because they feel too far out of your comfort zone. An example might be that you have always had a secret hankering to be an actor and, even though there is an amateur dramatic society in your area, you feel too shy to approach them. Well, this is where you must pull on your big girl/boy pants and decide that you are just going to be bold and go for it! It would be easy to adopt the mindset that you are too old to try new things but the more you push back against this attitude and take the brave step forward then the easier it will become and the more enjoyable and varied your life will be.

The second list requires you to list the types of cause where you feel you could help make a difference in the world. Many of us think that having the wherewithal to buy whatever luxury we want will lead to happiness but we usually find that the pleasure is short-lived. On the other hand, if we do more things which focus on helping others – whether through formal volunteering or just helping family and friends – we find that this takes our minds off our own troubles and can be a route to a deeper form of happiness.

Whichever cause you feel drawn to will tie in with your core values. For example, if you are an animal lover you may like to volunteer at a dog shelter. If poverty in society concerns you then you could volunteer in a charity shop or food bank. The scope for volunteering is huge so there should be something to suit everyone and the charities in question will be very grateful for your contribution.

At the end of this chapter, I am going to list a variety of activities which may give you some ideas for things you might like to try.

If you feel that your budget in retirement is going to be pretty tight, you could look at various ways to earn some extra cash. One idea, as I have mentioned before, is to work part-time. Even one or two days per week will bring in some welcome income. As an added bonus, studies suggest that continuing in the workforce for as long as possible helps to stave off dementia. It also gives you a continued purpose and, because you are interacting with others, boosts your mood and mental health.

You could start a small business selling your clutter on Ebay. Some people even trawl through charity shops, buy items with good re-saleable value, and sell them on at a profit. In 2017 the government agreed that a person can earn £1000 before they have to pay any tax but make sure you keep up to date with legislation.

It is now possible to write and publish a book - e-book or paperback - absolutely free of charge. So, if this has always been one of your ambitions, now is the time to give it a go. There are lots of tutorials on YouTube outlining the whole process.

One way to generate ideas for a small business is to think about your own interests. Someone who loves baking could approach local cafes or tea rooms to see if they would be interested in buying some of their produce. Or, they could concentrate their efforts on niche products such as wedding or celebration cakes. Again, make sure that you adhere to any relevant regulations. If you are an expert in your local places of interest you could start guided walking or cycling tours.

These are just some examples of ideas to help you boost your income. Not only will this type of activity help your finances but it will also give you an interesting new hobby.

Once you have an idea of the different activities you are interested in taking up, try to work out a routine for yourself. This can help eliminate any boredom that can come with a sudden excess of free time. If you have a partner, get them on board with this. Figure out activities you can do together and also some that you do individually. This gives you both something interesting to talk about and helps you avoid feelings of irritation towards each other which can be caused by too much togetherness – particularly if you have not been used to spending so much time in each other's company.

So, to sum up, you can see that your horizons can be expanded in all directions during retirement without the need for deep pockets. There is no need to sit at home bored to death – you just need to open your mind to all the exciting possibilities that await!

Below is a list of activities to give you some ideas of things you might like to try. They are divided into categories.

Physical Activities

Walking/running

Go Dancing

Yoga/Pilates

Play Tennis

Climb a Mountain

Swimming

Kayaking

Ride a Bicycle

Tai Chi

Gardening

Bowling

Badminton

Learn Something New

Learn a Language

Learn to Code

Research Your Family Tree

Learn to Knit/Sew

Take Cookery Lessons

Learn Flower Arranging

Learn How to Service Your Car

Grow Your Own Vegetables

Learn to Play Chess

Learn Photography

Go to Creative Writing Classes

Go to Art Classes

Learn Calligraphy

Volunteer

Work in a Charity Shop

Help Out at a Food Bank

Teach Literacy Classes

Join the Samaritans

Sit with an Elderly Person

Do Conservation Work

Join Your Parish Committee

Volunteer at a Hospice

Drive People to Hospital Appointments

Become a National Trust Guide

Creative Pursuits

Write a Book

Draw/Paint

Bake

Write a Song

Interior Design

Choreograph a Dance

Write Jokes

Design Clothes

Do Floral Arrangements

Relaxing Pursuits

Read a Book

Meditate

Do Stretching Exercises

Watch T.V.

Go to the Cinema

Nap

Listen to Music

Do Crossword Puzzles

Join a Historical Society

Go Fishing

Start a Small Business

Dog-walking

Write Wedding Invitations

Sell Stuff on Ebay

Start a YouTube

 Channel

Teach Exercise for Seniors

Start a B&B

Walking Tours of Your Local Area

Read Tarot Cards

Dressmaking

Mow Lawns

These are just some ideas to try – see how many
more you can think of.

CHAPTER 4
YOUR HEALTH IS YOUR WEALTH

The title of this chapter says it all. Even if you are very comfortably off financially, it is difficult to enjoy retirement if you are in poor health.

Many people will already be dealing with ongoing health issues but, in this chapter, I want to speak to those of us who are undermining our health with bad habits and how we might address changing these habits in a positive way.

This might perhaps be easier to do if we were like wealthy celebrities who can employ private chefs and personal trainers. However, we can achieve the same outcomes ourselves without the need to throw lots of money at the problem. The added bonus of this is that we can feel proud of our endeavors because we will not be taking the easy option.

We are bombarded with health advice from medical experts and media commentators. Unfortunately, much of the focus is on how badly behaved we are – the not-so-subtle disapproval if we should so much as look at a biscuit or glass of wine! For many of us this idea that we can hit a switch and will immediately find it easy to drop all our comforting habits and become instant paragons of virtue is wide off the mark. Rather than motivating us to change our habits it has quite the opposite effect. We feel that we fall so far short of achieving what is required to reach peak physical perfection that we just ignore the advice and continue to indulge ourselves without restraint. For some of us there can come a point where we feel guilty with all this self-indulgence. Maybe it is the New Year and we make resolutions to cut out all junk food and alcohol as well as starting a couch to 5K programme. We try to muster all the willpower and determination we have but, because we are trying to make too many changes at once, our good intentions soon fall by the wayside. We make up with our three best friends – the fridge, the sofa and the T.V.!

When we are working our days may be stressful and busy so when evening comes, all we feel able to do is slump in front of the T.V. with a takeaway and a glass or two of vino and one of our main excuses is that we do not have time for cooking or exercising. When we retire this situation can become worse rather than better because, even though we may have more time on our hands, if we do not have a plan on how best to use this time, we can become more and more demotivated. It is a vicious circle and we need to make a firm decision that all of this is going to change.

I suggest a two-pronged approach. The first step is to work on creating new purpose in your life. A more interesting life with varied activities will, hopefully, lead you away from spending the majority of your time eating, drinking and lazing about. Refer back to the last chapter to get started on your new get-a-life program.

I would advise having a health check-up with your doctor to ensure there are no underlying problems before you embark on a new health kick. Once you get a green light from your doctor the easiest way to make positive health changes is to take one small step at a time towards your goals.

Start a food diary and record all your food and drinks for two weeks. Look at your habits and work out small tweaks you could make that would be relatively painless. For example, if you normally have two chocolate digestives with your afternoon tea, have one plain digestive instead. Introduce these changes one at a time – for instance, make this your only change for a week and then next week add another. Educate yourself about healthy eating and list all the healthy foods that you really like and think about introducing the good things into your diet rather than depriving yourself.

Try to stop eating mindlessly or by the clock and eat only when you are hungry. You will notice that the first few bites of your food taste best and the pleasure diminishes as the meal goes on. It is a good idea to stop when you feel pleasantly full and the food stops tasting good – not when your plate is empty! Many of us have lost touch with hunger so you may need to eat more slowly and pay attention to your feelings of fullness. You may find that you will lose some weight by eating this way rather than going on a strict diet. If you prefer, you could set yourself small goals – for instance you could aim to lose 5lbs but do not set a time limit on reaching it. Just keep working steadily towards your goal and once you have achieved it you can set another one.

Moving our bodies has so many benefits for all aspects of our wellbeing including our mental health. Indeed, studies have shown that regular exercise can be as beneficial as anti-depressants for some milder forms of depression.

We can have a mental barrier where exercise is concerned and think that we have to spend hours in the gym or take up some strenuous activity such as running for it to count as exercise. There can be many reasons why we convince ourselves that it is just not for us. Perhaps we are carrying some extra weight and think we will make a fool of ourselves by running round the neighborhood or we may think that we are too old to start an exercise regime. Maybe we just feel completely unmotivated and want to take the path of least resistance. Once again, I recommend baby steps. If we start too vigorously, we may exhaust ourselves and vow to never try that again!

The easiest, not to mention, cheapest option is walking. You can just put on comfortable walking shoes, step through your front door and begin. On YouTube there are many walk-at-home tutorials which are a great way to ease you in gently. Indeed, YouTube has a huge range of exercise tutorials in everything from dance to yoga, tai chi to Pilates etc. The beauty of this for the budget conscious is that many of them are completely free of charge.

Whichever exercise program you start with, set yourself small but regular goals and slowly increase your activity. Make this more fun by teaming up with a partner or friend. Once you feel a bit fitter and more confident you could consider joining a group – maybe a hiking or cycling club or maybe you could start going to local dances. Often there are concession fees for those of us over 55. By taking up an active hobby like this you will not only be improving your health but you will also widen your social circle and will, hopefully, be enjoying yourself so much that exercise will no longer feel like a chore.

Try to keep more active in general with things like housework and gardening. The less time you spend sitting down, the better it is for your health.

For many of us any change in our routine, even if it is a positive change, can be stressful. We are creatures of habit. Often, we are unprepared for retirement and can find ourselves floundering in our new circumstances. Perhaps we hated our jobs and were eagerly awaiting the day we could pull the plug on our working lives but still find these changes hard to adapt to. We can feel that we have lost our identity along with our job title. This can lead to some problems with our mental health and is one of the reasons that it is good to have a plan in place for how we are going to spend our time in our retirement. If you are suffering from a low mood rather than a more serious condition then, hopefully, the suggestions in this book will be helpful in alleviating this whether by improving your nutrition and exercise or giving you ideas on how to form a new routine.

If your mental health issues are more serious then it is imperative that you seek help. Your doctor should be your first port of call as they have the tools and advice you need. Some people still feel that there is a stigma attached to mental health problems and think that they have to maintain a stiff upper lip and battle on themselves but having a mental health malady is just the same as suffering from any physical ailment and I am sure you would not hesitate to consult your doctor if you had sustained something like a broken leg so, please do not suffer in silence.

Keeping your brain active is important as you age. Consider learning to meditate as it can provide many benefits to your general health and state of mind.

Again, many of the ideas in this book can be helpful in sharpening your brainpower. Eating well and exercising, learning something new and interacting socially have been shown to help you retain good cognitive function. The brain likes to be challenged and, even though we do not know for sure whether any of this can help prevent dementia, there is no doubt that keeping your brain active will improve its everyday capabilities.

Getting enough sleep is another important factor in maintaining good health. Without an adequate amount of sleep, you will not have the energy to take up more active pursuits and the fact is that the more active you are the more energy you will have so it is important that you develop a good sleep routine. Try to go to bed and rise at roughly the same time each day. Have a wind-down routine before you go to bed – for example, having a bath, turning off all screens at least an hour before bed, reading a book, drinking some cocoa or chamomile tea – will help to relax you and prepare you for a restful sleep. If you are lying in bed wide awake and tossing and turning, then it is better to get up and read for a while until you feel sleepy. If you continue to have problems with insomnia consult your doctor for more advice.

Hopefully, this chapter will have given you some pointers on how to make small, sustainable changes to your health-related habits. You can take baby steps which are still within your comfort zone and build on them bit by bit. This will make the whole process less daunting and you will therefore be much more likely to stick with it. You will be rewarded with much more energy and zest for life – what could be better than that?

The Finale

So, there you have it folks. This book is intended as a starter course on how to enjoy a fulfilling retirement without needing bucket loads of cash. We need to realize that most of our joy in life does not come from having thousands sitting in our bank account, even though that would be quite pleasant. Our main asset can be our creative brainpower and I am hoping that some of the ideas I have given you will inspire you to come up with ingenious ways of making those thousands if that is what you would like to achieve but, in any event, applying ourselves and succeeding at goals we have set - whether they involve financial gain or not – will give us feelings of accomplishment and contentment. Money cannot buy those feelings.

Set yourself the task of seeing how varied, interesting and fun you can make your life in retirement. Invest in your relationships, both family and community and invest in yourself. I think you will find this way more fulfilling than spending and getting.

This is your challenge and I hope you choose to accept it. Good luck!

Occupational therapy
in the community